A PARENT'S *Survival* GUIDE
How to Cope When Your Kid is Using Drugs

Harriet W. Hodgson

Hazelden ®

First published August, 1986.

ISBN: 0-89486-390-8

Printed in the United States of America.

Editor's Note:
   Hazelden Educational Materials offers a variety of information on chemical dependency and related areas. Our
publications do not necessarily represent Hazelden or its
programs, nor do they officially speak for any Twelve Step
organization.

CONTENTS

Introduction

This book is intended as a quick reference for parents, a guide to help you survive your child's chemical dependency. I didn't plan to write it. However, relatives, friends, and total strangers gradually changed my mind.

People approach me in stores, after church, on elevators. Some call at the crack of dawn. They frequently ask two questions:

"How did you know you had a child using drugs?"

"What did you do about it?"

One day a friend called to ask if I'd meet with a friend of hers. "She has a son using drugs and needs someone to talk to," I was told. I met with her friend. As we chatted over coffee I handed her a hastily scribbled list of pitfalls to avoid. A year later I met this mother again. Her face lit up when she saw me. "I carried your list in my purse since you gave it to me," she said. "It helped me survive."

That's what this book is about. It's a written version of what I've been saying. I've talked about chemical dependency to church groups, parent groups, and neighborhood groups. This is not a comprehensive resource or a Ph.D. thesis; it isn't meant to imply I am an expert on the subject. It is, however, based upon experience.

This book is purposely a paperback. It's designed to travel with you. You can toss it into your briefcase or backpack, or carry it in your car. Features include an easy-to-read style and clear headings to help you find your way. For a quick glimpse, read chapters two and eight first. THE SYMPTOMS CHAPTER CAN SAVE YOUR CHILD. THE PITFALLS CHAPTER CAN SAVE YOU.

Chapter 1: Defining Chemical Dependency

WHAT ARE CHEMICALS?

Physicians and treatment professionals define chemicals as any substances which alter bodily functions and responses. The National Institute on Drug Abuse classifies these substances as

- Opiates
- Depressants
- Stimulants
- Hallucinogens and Anticholinergics
- Cannabinoids
- Dissociative Anesthetics

Since foods and industrial substances can alter bodily functions and responses, they are also classified as chemicals. It's possible to get stoned on nutmeg or aerosol cooking oil. Or, a person can get stoned on such industrial compounds as glue, dry-cleaning fluid, and typewriter correction fluid.

Alcohol, the primary drug of choice for teenagers, is classified as a chemical. By the time they've graduated, 93 percent of the high school students have tried alcohol and 69 percent have used in the prior month.[1] Studies conducted by the National Institute on Drug Abuse reveal binge drinking among teenagers at a "disturbingly high level."

Nicotine, too, is classified as a chemical. Government surveys of senior high school students show that "cigarettes are used daily by more of the respondents (21 percent) than any of the other drug classes."[2] Public health officials are particularly upset about the surge in smoking among teenage girls.

Cigarette smoking is now the biggest cancer killer of women in the United States. Putting cigarettes and alcohol together causes even more problems since it appears that each increases the health threats of the other.[3]

WHAT IS CHEMICAL DEPENDENCY?

In its publication, *Testing Drugs for Physical Dependence Potential and Abuse Liability*, the National Institute on Drug Abuse is careful to separate physical dependence from abuse.

> Physical dependence . . . refers to physiological and behavioral alterations that become increasingly manifest when drug administration is stopped *after* repeated exposure to a pharmacologic agent. . . . Abuse is used with reference to events that *precede* or accompany strong drug-seeking, drug discrimination, and drug-taking behaviors in association with self-administration of a pharmacological agent.[4]

In general, treatment centers consider chemical dependency to mean dependency upon chemicals in order to "function." Function is in quotation marks because it deviates from the normal definition. You may well ask if the chemically dependent person is functioning at all, because his or her life revolves around drugs, including alcohol.

A study of cocaine users states, "The most striking feature of this pattern is that the drug use dominates the individual's life and precludes other social functioning."[5]

Research shows chemically dependent people exhibit four common traits: (1) They have an overwhelming urge to get stoned repeatedly. (2) This urge is stronger than innate or learned needs. (3) The urge to get stoned is automatic — it triggers itself. (4) Getting stoned "becomes so deeply imbedded or indelibly etched within the person's experience that it can never be consciously or unconsciously 'forgotten.'"[6]

Chapter 2: How Do You Know If Your Child Is Chemically Dependent?

Even well-educated people fail to recognize chemical dependency. Why? They may be uninformed about chemical dependency, they may underestimate the degree of use, or they may be too close to the problem. And, "bright kids use all their intelligence to deceive parents," a psychiatrist explains.

Symptoms of adolescent chemical dependency are difficult to sort out from normal behavior. Most teenagers prepare to "leave the nest" by questioning, acting out, arguing, and asserting their independence. But it's excessive behavior which may flag chemical dependency, says Dr. George Comerci, chief of adolescent/young adult medicine, at the University of Arizona Health Sciences Center in Tucson. "Mood swings [are] more pronounced than those teenagers usually experience," reports Dr. Comerci. He also notes "a rebellious and paranoid flavor to all interpersonal relationships with adults, siblings and authority figures."[1]

Dr. Comerci says young substance abusers progress through five stages. Stage one is the potential for abuse. Potential includes such factors as using parents, easy access to chemicals, low self-esteem, and personality disorders. Stage two is experimentation, a stage frequently minimized by users. Stage three is preoccupation with drugs, a time when youngsters buy all sorts of drug paraphernalia. Stage four is addiction — the addict's primary goal in life is to get stoned. Stage five is the logical result of addiction — physical and psychological deterioration.[2]

Substance abuse among youngsters doesn't occur just in high school. Use of alcohol and other drugs has filtered down to the elementary grades. In an eight-year study of drug use among senior high students, the government found almost ten percent of the class of 1983 started using alcohol in sixth grade. Slightly more than three percent of the class began smoking daily in sixth grade, and over three percent began smoking marijuana.[3]

PHYSICAL SYMPTOMS

A grade school student using pot might appear to have the flu. A senior high school student might tell parents, "I've got a cold." Don't fall for excuses. Be alert to physical symptoms that might be signs of stress, overwork, health problems, *or* of drug involvement:

- bloodshot eyes
- dull-looking eyes
- watering eyes
- drowsiness
- manic/hyper behavior
- runny nose
- coughing
- needle marks on arms
- weight loss
- constant desire for junk food
- malnutrition
- some forms of acute acne
- tremors
- hallucinations
- delusions

EMOTIONAL SYMPTOMS

If your child has been using drugs for some time, his or her emotional behavior has been altered. It's important to remember the child's value system is also altered. What was once important to your child may not be any longer.

At first your child may argue about one house rule. Arguments accelerate, with the child questioning most house rules. Finally, parents find themselves arguing with their child over almost everything.

"Why are we fighting about this?" you ask. "You know the rules."

From the parents' viewpoint, arguments over established rules are ridiculous, time-consuming, and exhausting. Their child's emotional outbursts make each day a hassle. What had once been a peaceful home is now a battleground.

Normal adolescent behavior can include similar outbursts and emotional scenes, a fact that makes it difficult for parents to identify their child's drug use. Parental suspicion should be aroused, though, if such behaviors occur in conjunction with physical symptoms or with these emotional symptoms:

- irresponsible behavior
- argumentative behavior (beyond what is normal adolescent rebellion)
- lack of motivation
- solitary behavior (staying in a room all day)
- constant desire to be away from home
- nonparticipation in family activities
- new, unusual friends
- forgetfulness
- lying
- changes in speaking patterns; rapid or slow speech
- legal problems (drunk driving, coming home drunk or high)

Spotting any of these signs may indicate a drug problem, but many young people experience difficulties without using drugs. The most important thing parents can do is talk to their children about feelings, concerns, or any problem they may be having. But before deciding that they are having drug problems, consult a counselor trained to recognize these types of problems.

OTHER SYMPTOMS

Later you may spot signs of chemical dependency you missed earlier. For example, your child may join "the jacket crowd." This group of students wears jackets in school all day using pockets to stash drugs. Other symptoms of chemical dependency are blatant. Still, parents overlook them, considering them isolated incidents. Be alert to these symptoms:

- drugs missing from medicine cabinet
- missing wine or liquor
- falling grades
- truancy
- car accidents
- missing clothing or possessions
- strange phone calls
- obsession with loud music
- fascination with flashing light displays
- inability to account for allowance or wages
- use of eye drops (clears redness from eyes)
- use of incense (masks the odor of pot)
- odd, small containers in pockets, purses, drawers
- white specks on nostrils or clothing (sniffing correction fluid)
- appointments at odd hours

The presence of a few of these behaviors does not constitute chemical dependency. Most young people are not chemically dependent. What counts is the total picture. If you have a gut feeling something is wrong, find yourself arguing excessively about ordinary things, and notice a marked difference in your child's health, it's possible he or she is using drugs.

Chapter 3: Available Drugs and Their Effects

SOURCES OF DRUGS

Young people have easy access to some harmful substances. A virtual potpourri of mind-altering substances is available.

Over-the-Counter Drugs

Young people can walk into any drug store and buy these products:

- analgesics
- antihistamines/allergy products
- antirheumatics
- bronchiodilators/asthma remedies
- cold remedies/cough syrup
- mouthwashes
- opthalmic products
- sedatives/sleep aids
- stimulants
- topical analgesics
- weight-reduction pills

Street Drugs

Street drugs are those which can be illegally purchased on the street or in school. "I can get anything I want in five minutes," boasts a junior in high school.

Local police departments can tell you which drugs are selling best during any given week. Law enforcement officials have seen two disturbing changes in street-drug sales. Cocaine is emerging as the top-selling street drug, and the manufacture of "designer drugs" is increasing.

Designer drugs, facsimilies of known drugs, are the result of "increasing sophistication of street-drug suppliers, who can now tailor their products to individual preferences regarding the nature and the duration of the 'high.' "[1] What young people don't realize is that designer drugs are impure, untested, and downright dangerous. Dr. J. William Langston of the Santa Clara Valley Medical Center says users of these drugs are "unwittingly serving as guinea pigs."

Langston describes his attempt to track down a designer drug heroin formula. "We went to the organic chemistry department library at Stanford University. It was eerie indeed to open a 1947 volume of *The Journal of Organic Chemistry* and find that the paper had been taken, cut out meticulously with a razor blade. We then went to the Stanford Medical Center in search of other papers from the 1940s, only to find that each article . . . had been removed in the same fashion. We seemed to be retracing the footsteps of an underground chemist, perhaps the one who had already ruined six lives."[2]

Constantly changing formulas, manufacturing sites, and terminology make it difficult for the law to catch underground chemists.

Drug Alterations

Drug use is further complicated by drug alterations. *How to Get Off Drugs* details four common alterations: (1) *dilution*, inactive substances are added to a drug to increase bulk and profits; (2) *adulteration*, the drug is cut with an inert ingredient such as caffeine; (3) *substitution*, production of look-alike capsules; (4) *contamination*, a great hazard to drug users, ". . . most often results when basement chemists get sloppy."[3]

Other variables, such as age, medical history, drug mixing, individual responses, and emotional responses also affect the body's response to chemicals.

ADDICTION THEORY

Scientists have hoped to find a universal addiction theory, one that would explain the addictive process in all afflicted people. Although neurochemistry is a long way from solving the addiction puzzle, some pieces are falling into place through opiate and alcohol research.

Researchers have discovered brain chemicals called endorphins, which are naturally occurring proteins. Their effects are similar to morphine and other opiates. Specific areas of the brain have nerve receptors for endorphins, and these brain sites may react similarly to opiates and endorphins.

Alcohol (and probably other sedatives) are changed into tetrahydroisoquinoline alkaloids (TIQs), which are related to endorphins. Therefore, it's possible that opiates and sedatives have at least one common chemical pathway affecting the brain. TIQs may be the common step in that pathway. Common pathways may be the reason some young people can switch drugs to satisfy cravings.

All users do not become addicted. Ninety-five percent of heroin users returning from Vietnam were able to stop using heroin. Of these, only sixteen percent became addicted again, and a majority of them responded favorably to treatment.[4]

Why do some become addicted?

1. *Heredity.* There's probably a hereditary factor involved in brain metabolism.

2. *Endorphin Deficiency.* Chemically dependent people may have a metabolic endorphin deficiency, which puts psychological and physiological demands on them to take more chemicals that generate endorphins.

3. *Endorphin Production.* When chemically dependent people use drugs, they may produce more endorphins than other people.

4. *More Receptors.* Chemically dependent people may have more endorphin receptors than others.

5. *Receptor Sensitivity.* These receptors may be more

sensitive in chemically dependent people, through TIQs or similar chemicals.

Although other drugs young people use haven't been studied as much as opiates and alcohol, almost all have been found to enter into brain metabolism through one of the known nerve transmission pathways. Neurochemical systems can only be considered superficially here. Bottom-line conclusions are these:

- Chemical dependency may be a hereditary and metabolic phenomenon.
- A chemically dependent person can't control his or her use of chemicals.
- Chemical dependency can be the cause of sudden personality changes or erratic behavior.
- Young people don't take chemicals in order to misbehave.
- It's difficult to change a chemically dependent person's behavior while he or she is using drugs. As a counselor summarized it: "You can't argue or bargain with a junkie."

These conclusions aren't meant to discount the psychiatric factors in chemical dependency. Chemically dependent young people often have psychiatric problems. These problems should be dealt with by a professional who has experience dealing with chemically dependent patients.

SPECIFIC DRUGS AND EFFECTS

Here are some handy facts on drugs and their effects. This is not intended as comprehensive information. Six general categories follow, and a seventh section briefly discusses ethyl alcohol.

Opiates

Examples

Heroin, Morphine, Codeine, Methadone, Meperidine (Demerol®), Pentazocine (Talwin®), Hydromorphone

12

(Dilaudid®), Opium (Paregoric), MPPP and MPTP (designer drugs)

Effects
Opiates cause sleep and reduce pain. These drugs are abused because of pleasurable stimulation to certain brain centers. Users feel a "rush" just after use. Opiates also cause nausea, vomiting, restlessness, unconsciousness, cessation of breathing, and death. Pinpoint eye pupils can be a telltale sign of opiate use.

Comments
Heroin is the most abused opiate. It's potent, easy to manufacture (from opium), and easy to sell in small packages. MPPP is a "designer drug" that is often contaminated with MPTP. Contamination causes a severe brain disease, similar to Parkinson's. It should be noted that many opiates have legitimate medical uses. Withdrawal symptoms are very severe. Methadone is often used for treatment of opiate addiction (Methadone maintenance).

Depressants (sedatives, volatile anesthetics, antihistamines)

Examples of Sedatives
Barbiturates: (Seconal®, Nembutal®, Tuinal®, Carbrital®)
Nonbarbiturates: (Noctec®, Equanil®, Miltown®, Librium®, Valium®, Doriden®, bromides, and many others)

Examples of Volatile Anesthetics
Anesthetics: (alcohol, ether, halogenated anesthetic gases such as halothane, nitrous oxide, chloroform)
Organic Solvents: (alcohols, ketones, benzenes, toluenes, esthers, glycols, and gasoline)

Examples of Antihistamines
Benadryl®, Chlor-Trimeton®, many cold and allergy medicines, Tagamet®, and Zantac®

Effects
All depressants cause euphoria, relaxation, and decreased inhibition in lower doses. Slightly higher doses can lead to

uncoordinated motion, a staggering walk, poor judgment, poor reflexes, unconsciousness, and even death.

Comments

1. Sedatives — calming, tranquilizing drugs — are prescribed in lower doses as tranquilizers. All tranquilizers are really sedatives.
2. Organic solvents can be found anywhere and everywhere — in glue, aerosol products, painting products, cleaning products, and degreasing fluids, to name a few.
3. Antihistamines cause drowsiness in low doses, hallucinations in higher doses.
4. Withdrawal from barbiturates and alcohol can be *lethal*. Therefore, withdrawal must be carried out under strict medical supervision.

Stimulants

Examples

Cocaine, amphetamines, Ritalin®, caffeine, theophyllin, ephedrin, and phenylpropanolamine

Effects

Stimulants cause a feeling of increased alertness and physical activity. Users feel some euphoria at first. However, these stimulants also cause erratic increases in heart rate and blood pressure. Other effects of stimulants include dry mouth, sweating, anxiety, flushed face, various tremors, and loss of coordination. Higher doses cause sudden excessive high blood pressure, high fever, heart failure, and stroke. Long-term effects include kidney damage, depression, and brain damage.

Comments

1. Cocaine is a short-lived stimulant. A person dependent on it may need frequent and expensive doses to avoid severe "letdown" and depression.
2. Amphetamines were once used as appetite suppressants. Now this use is outlawed. The only legal uses are in treatment of narcolepsy and as antidotes for overdoses of depressants.

Hallucinogens and Anticholinergics (Psychedelics)

Examples
LSD, mescaline (peyote), psilocybin (mushroom), atropine, and scopolamine

Effects
These drugs can cause moderate to severe changes in perception, sensations, and thinking. Ultimately, they result in auditory or visual hallucinations. The user can swing rapidly from one emotion to another. Pupils dilate. There are increases in heart rate, temperature, and blood pressure. Users may also experience loss of appetite, tremors, and sweating.

Comments
Hallucinogens can cause rapid and extreme changes in mood, emotion, and perceptions. These can be frightening and lead to "bad trips." Some can lead to flashbacks, during which the drugs effects are experienced again although they have not been taken again.

Cannabinoids

Effects
Marijuana is used for the initial feeling of euphoria. Other effects include impairment of memory, altered sense of time, loss of concentration, loss of coordination, and impairment of reflexes. Long-term effects include amotivational syndrome (see Chapter 5: Boredom) and severe preoccupation with the drug. Reported effects on hormones and the reproductive organs may be worse in adolescence when the reproductive system is developing.

Comments
Young people often don't remember what they learn while using marijuana. Driving under the influence of marijuana is hazardous. Many substances sold on the street as marijuana are phony vegetable materials treated with LSD or PCP.

Examples
Marijuana, hashish, and THC

Dissociative Anesthetics

Examples

PCP (phencyclidine and ketamine)

Effects

PCP has a very complex effect on the brain. It causes the brain to be "disassociated" from pain and other perceptions. Small doses cause increases in heart rate, blood pressure, and sweating. Dizziness, numbness, and hallucinations occur as the dosage increases. Large doses can lead to convulsions, stroke, heart failure, and death.

Comments

Very little PCP comes from legitimate drug manufacturers. Most PCP is made in illicit "kitchen chemistry labs." On the street, PCP is often poorly made, impure, and contaminated with other related compounds such as PCC, which releases cyanide and is considered very poisonous.

Additional Notes About Ethyl Alcohol

An organic solvent, alcohol turns into an aldehyde in the body. Alcohol is an anesthetic which has some of the same effects on the brain as opiates. The dose of alcohol which causes extreme intoxication or unconsciousness is very close to the dose which causes death. Withdrawal can lead to a whole spectrum of severe central nervous system effects, including convulsions and death.

Chapter 4: Facing Reality

GOVERNMENT STATISTICS ON DRUG USE

Facing the reality of chemical dependency means facing the statistics. In *Drugs and American High School Students 1975-1983*, the National Institute on Drug Abuse reported the results of a survey of the class of 1983. These twelfth grade students were asked to disclose their own and their friends' use of drugs. The following charts show these differences.

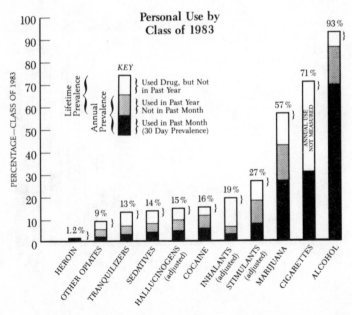

NOTES: The bracket near the top of a bar indicates the lower and upper limits of the 95% confidence interval.

17

The results, theoretically, should have been similar. The three most-used substances in both reporting methods were alcohol, cigarettes, and marijauna; heroin was the least-used according to both. However, there was a significant difference between the percentages of self-admitted users and of friends who use.

Why the difference? I suspect it is due to the way the study was conducted. Many students won't be honest in listing their chemical use on a questionnaire, but they may be more honest in reporting about their friends' usage. Perhaps they even list their own use in the friends' category.

If your child is using drugs, he or she will be no more honest with you about that use than these students were in answering this questionnaire. Your response, once you are convinced that alcohol or other drug use is a problem for your child, should be decisive and positive. Chemical dependency can be a fatal

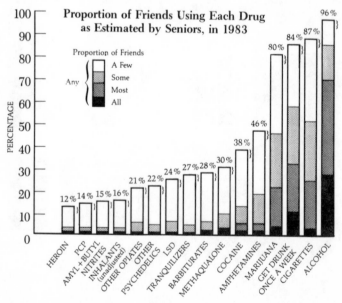

NOTES: The bracket near the top of a bar indicates the lower and upper limits of the 95% confidence interval.

disease, and your child's life may be at stake. It is imperative to act quickly. If your child is using chemicals, don't delay. DO SOMETHING!

Don't waste time on
- self-pity (You can feel that later — if you must.)
- anger (Channel this energy into something positive.)
- explanations (They don't change what happened.)
- guilt (A guilt-ridden parent is an ineffective parent.)
- family bickering (Bickering yields nothing.)

CONFRONTING YOUR CHILD

If the evidence is becoming too great to ignore, it's time to confront your child. Your goal is to help the addict help him- or herself.

Do your homework before confrontation. Get four pieces of paper. On the first piece, list the physical and emotional symptoms you have observed. On the second, list what you believe to be the effects of drug use — car crashes, health problems, falling grades. On the third, list words which describe how you are feeling. Use simple words such as scared, anxious, angry, and hurt. On the fourth, list harmful consequences of drug using. These can include memory loss, inability to solve problems, and physical harm. Keep these lists for reference.

Pick the best time for you to confront your child. Allow time for a two-way discussion. Here are some confrontation tips:
- Talk to your child when he or she isn't stoned, if possible. You can't reason with chemicals or booze.
- Talk honestly. Use simple, straight-forward language. If your child has been using drugs for some time, detailed explanations, intellectual terms, even logical reasoning may not "compute."
- Talk without anger — probably one of your biggest challenges.
- Describe observations only. Leave out sarcasm and "poor me" stories.

- Describe harmful consequences of using. Be specific.
- Propose you seek help — together.

Your child is scared. Scared of his or her peer group, scared of being labeled a nerd, and scared of brain damage. If ever there was a time your child needed you, it is NOW.

Chapter 5: How Did This Happen?

You're probably asking yourself, "How did this happen?" or "Where did I go wrong?" Such questions are a natural part of parental shock.

A variety of factors can contribute to chemical dependency: family history, family roles, boredom, lack of coping skills, ignorance, experimentation, and peer pressure.

FAMILY HISTORY

How many of your family members could be classified as chemically dependent? The answer may surprise you. Was good old Uncle Roger always smashed at family functions? Did Aunt Minnie "tipple"? It might be helpful to draw a diagram of your family tree and see how many family members abuse alcohol or other drugs or who are chemically dependent.

FAMILY ROLES

Family roles influence how a person responds to alcohol and other drugs. Don Wegscheider, author of *If Only My Family Understood Me . . .* , categorizes family roles as

- protector — a person close to the victim
- caretaker — often works with the protector (and works harder than ever during the crisis)
- problem child — seeks attention during the crisis
- forgotten child — takes care of self (to the relief of harried parents)
- family pet — uses humor to relieve situations

- professional enabler — usually not part of the household, the person who can really foul things up

Wegscheider diagrams interaction between family members with triangles. Many triangular combinations are possible, complicating family life and its response to crisis. And of course, no one fits neatly or perfectly into one or a combination of these roles.

BOREDOM

In a world filled with things to do and see, it's amazing to hear our children say, "I'm bored." Some parents may even encourage this feeling of boredom with statements such as, "Those teachers really are dumb," or "Yeah, this is a small town."

One study suggests that boredom is one reason some college students use pot: "Frequent marijuana smokers reported more often than infrequent smokers that being bored was the problem."[1]

The problem becomes self-perpetuating since a child spaced-out on drugs is bound to be bored. This once-active child will spend hours staring at TV. Occasionally, the child might comment about the day's plans, but he or she still stares straight ahead, doing nothing. This is called amotivational behavior; unmotivated children move through life in slow motion. They display no self-starting traits, don't pursue projects, or make long-term plans. The behavior is curious in that, from the child's viewpoint, he or she feels things are being accomplished.

LACK OF COPING SKILLS

Teenagers are just getting to know themselves as they enter high school: interests, career goals, likes, and dislikes. Self-knowledge coupled with maturity gives kids coping skills. Some examples of coping skills are

- verbalizing feelings

- identifying feelings (anger, fear, and loneliness)
- developing new interests
- improving old interests
- deferring judgment until more information is available
- setting goals
- selecting social situations which offer few or no temptations

Teenagers without coping skills are perfect candidates for drug use. Such children have difficulty saying no or thinking of alternative choices. Chemical dependency treatment helps them develop coping skills.

IGNORANCE

Some parents of chemically dependent children are astonished at their own ignorance of chemical addiction. They shouldn't be, because the ignorance factor is usually long-term and twofold. First, they are ignorant about a child's experimentation with drugs. Second, they are ignorant about today's drugs and their effects. You're not the first parent to be ignorant about chemical dependency.

Parents are often the last people to learn their child is using drugs. This is because parents have been fooled. Their child has worked hard to maintain normal behavior, getting decent, sometimes outstanding grades, and participating in a variety of school activities. Home behavior focuses on not arousing parental suspicion.

A child using drugs creates a ripple effect in the community. Peer group members, in the middle of the ripple, know your child is using. Perhaps the youngsters are even using together. Children tell concurrent stories, matching times, places, and incidents to mask drug use. As parents, you are not at the center and have no idea what is going on.

Strangers, on the outer edge of the ripple, are often parents of peer group children. These parents know your child is using, might not know *their* child is using, and face a terrible dilemma. Should they call you to report suspicions based upon fragmentary evidence?

Actually, parents and children are both ignorant. Teenagers, filled with the optimism of youth, feel chemical dependency won't happen to them. They view themselves as experimenters imbued with some sort of magical immunity. "I can handle using," they tell each other. At the same time, parents — many of whom came from a generation that didn't use drugs — are oblivious to the drug pressures their children face.

Parents confronted with the ignorance factor also confront self-doubt. "Would we have caught it sooner if we'd been better informed?" partners ask each other. This is followed by the gut-wrenching question, "Have we been good parents?" Although both questions are logical, the answers don't matter. Worrying about ignorance doesn't change what happened.

EXPERIMENTATION

Some parents play mental games. They say, "Oh, she's just using a little pot." Unfortunately, this excuse disregards medical evidence. A little pot can become a lot, or it can lead to use of other drugs. A 1981 study of 2,510 males, all in their twenties, showed that about ten percent of the 1,382 pot-users also used heroin, but only one man of the remaining 1,128 used heroin. In citing this study, author Peggy Mann points out that most of the frequent heroin users were heavy pot users. She adds, "The greater the extent of marijuana use, the greater the chance that one will use other drugs."[2]

Some effects of pot smoking are what you'd expect, such as cancerous lesions to lungs. Other effects may surprise you. Mann says they include

- psychological dependence
- diminished willpower, concentration, attention span, ability to deal with abstract ideas, and low tolerance for frustration
- decrease in oxygen which reaches the heart

- reduced sperm count
- abnormal sperm

What does this mean? It means parents shouldn't fall for the experimentation ploy. TAKE A STAND AGAINST DRUGS.

PEER INFLUENCE

All other reasons for chemical dependency pale against peer influence. "A comparison with the senior's own attitudes regarding drug use reveals that on the average they are much more in accord with their peers than with their parents," reports an eight-year government study by the U.S. Department of Health and Human Services.[3]

In an effort to combat peer influence the department initiated its "Just Say No" campaign. Carol Sussman, campaign coordinator, says it is aimed at elementary children in the hope of deterring them from using. Television ad spots feature a boy who looks only about eight years old.

Certainly, today's kids feel pressure. If your kid gets in the wrong crowd, receives a dare, or is caught between crowds, he or she really feels it. Some physicians and treatment counselors feel the media have provided their own kind of pressure by communicating so well, so instantly, the facts about drug use and thereby increasing curiosity and, possibly, experimentation.[4]

Ask parents of chemically dependent children, and they'll tell you peer pressure can undermine parenting. Parental efforts, dedication, sacrifice, and role models quiver against the gale of peer pressure.

How can this happen? Three reasons. First, by sheer numbers. A child has more peers than parents. Second, youngsters tend to spend more time with their peers than with their parents. And finally, all of us — child or adult — wish to be accepted by others in our approximate age group.

Chapter 6: Which Treatment Is Best?

Minnesota has been one of the pioneers in chemical dependency treatment. Chemical dependency counselors refer to the state's treatment options as The Minnesota Model. Perhaps your state has more available help than you think.

FINDING HELP

Check the yellow pages, newspaper, TV, and radio ads for information on treatment centers in your area. Help should be available from

- Alcoholics Anonymous (A.A.)
- Narcotics Anonymous (N.A.)
- Al-Anon
- Nar-Anon
- state treatment centers
- private treatment centers
- hospitals
- crisis centers
- county services: social services, family violence committees
- 1-800-Cocaine

Help is just a phone call away. A startling number of people have received help from 800-Cocaine, for example. In the first year and a half of its existence, more than 450,000 calls were received.[1]

TREATMENT TYPES

It is impossible to give in-depth descriptions of treatment types here. However, brief definitions are still helpful. Basic types of treatment are Gestalt treatment, Alcoholics Anonymous, transactional analysis, cognitive therapy, and self-control groups.

Gestalt Treatment

Gestalt is a German word which means whole. Treatment focuses on making the individual self-reliant. Modern psychiatry uses many Gestalt techniques. These include "role playing, exaggeration of symptoms or behavior, use of fantasy, and the principle of staying with the immediate moment . . . use of the word *I* rather than *it* as a way to assume responsibility for behavior, learning how to talk *to* rather than *at* someone, becoming aware of bodily senses, and learning to 'stay with feelings' until they are understood and integrated."[2]

Alcoholics Anonymous

A.A. is based upon one premise — total abstinence. Many physicians and chemical dependency counselors feel A.A. is the only treatment that works. Certainly, A.A. has developed a good track record since its founding in 1935 by a New York businessman visiting Akron, Ohio. Today A.A. is a worldwide movement with groups in 114 countries. Membership is over one million.

Working through A.A.'s Twelve Steps helps alcoholics deal with their drinking problems and maintain sobriety. No dues are required, although members may make contributions. Visitors are welcome to attend open meetings. Sometimes local chapters have special groups for young people and professionals. Anonymity is always maintained.

Many treatment centers base their programs on the principles of A.A. using a multidisciplinary approach. These programs focus on the individual's physical, psychological, emotional, social, and spiritual health. Patients are introduced to the Twelve Steps of A.A. and to A.A. as an aftercare source.

Transactional Analysis

TA uses analysis of transactions as a basis for changing behavior. Dr. Eric Berne explains, "First the analysis of simple transactions, then the analysis of a stereotyped series of transactions, and finally the analysis of long, complex operations often involving several people and usually based upon rather elaborate fantasies."[3] Berne uses the rescue fantasy example of the woman who marries one alcoholic after another.

With TA everyone has three ego states: parent, adult, and child. Treatment works best in groups because "the group serves as a setting in which people can become more aware of themselves, the structure of their individual personalities, how they transact with others, the games they play, and the scripts they act out."[4] What are transactions? Daily relationships between people. Structural analysis refers to individual personality. Transactional analysis refers to conversations and actions. Game analysis refers to behavior which yields a payoff. Script analysis is — you guessed it — life's dramas.[5]

Cognitive Therapy

Although methods differ, cognitive therapists "agree that changing maladaptive thought patterns is central to the therapeutic effort."[6]

One cognitive therapist is Dr. David Burns, who continued the mood research done by Dr. Aaron Beck at the University of Pennsylvania during the mid-fifties. Dr. Burns says, "The first principle of cognitive therapy is that *all* your moods are created by your 'cognitions,' or thoughts. . . . The second principle is that when you are feeling depressed, your thoughts are dominated by pervasive negativity. . . . The third principle is of enormous philosophical and therapeutic importance. Our research has documented that the negative thoughts which cause your emotional turmoil nearly *always* contain gross distortions."[7]

Cognitive therapy uses individual counseling, role playing,

assessments, daily records, and checklists to help patients modify their moods.

Self-Control Groups

Self-control groups are springing up all across the country. You've probably read their ads inducing people to conquer fears, stop smoking, or lose weight. These groups encourage clients to set their own goals; the therapist functions as a consultant.[8]

Group members use three steps to achieve goals. The steps involve behavior modification. First, good behavior is rewarded; negative behavior is not. Second, rewards are earned only if the desired behavior occurs. Third, group members take steps to control their environment, in essence, stacking the odds in their favor. A dieter, for example, will load the refrigerator with slimming foods.

Self-help group members work independently. There might be regularly scheduled pep meetings to perk up members. However, "therapists serve as advisors and intervene only when needed."[9]

Other

Various organizations are trying to help young people stop using drugs. This is a noble aim, but investigate these groups carefully. Good intentions cannot replace competence. Research any group or organization to be sure such dangerous practices as sleep deprivation, malnutrition, and neurotic obedience are not used.

COMPARISONS

Do some basic research before you select a treatment center. Compare facilities by cost, staff qualifications, and appropriateness.

Cost

Treatment can be very expensive. Get a concept of costs now

to avoid surprises later. Some treatment centers charge sliding fees according to income. Costs include

- initial costs
- room and board (Get a dollar per day figure.)
- professional fees
- transportation fees
- additional fees (These can include medications, craft supplies, textbooks, and workbooks.)

Unfortunately, many insurance companies are saying they will only cover the cost of outpatient treatment. In reply, reliable centers say the only treatment that really works best is inpatient treatment. Insurance payment policies are changing so call your local insurance agent for the latest information.

If your child has been ordered, by the courts, to go through treatment, some of the costs may be absorbed by county or state government.

Staff Qualifications

Select a facility that has a well-trained, qualified staff. In order to become licensed as a Chemical Dependency Practitioner, the University of Minnesota requires 51 course credits, plus 1,000 hours of internship. Hours must be spent in different areas. Examples: prevention/intervention, assessment/aftercare, and inpatient treatment.

Don't be afraid to ask for credentials. A good treatment facility has fully qualified physicians (including psychiatrists) and nurses. Counselors, sometimes called practitioners, are licensed by the state. Student counselors should be carefully supervised. Treatment centers frequently hire counselors who are recovering. These recovering chemically dependent people are good role models, can spot con games, relate to chemically dependent people well, and can be effective intermediaries between staff and patients.[10]

Appropriateness

Finally, match the appropriateness of the facility to your

child's needs. If possible, choose a nearby facility because it will be more convenient.

And answer these questions:

1. Is the facility clean? The facility should be clean enough to meet medical standards. And it should be attractive and well maintained.
2. Does the facility have a good reputation? After all, a good reputation is the best form of advertising.
3. Does the facility offer elementary school/high school classes? This is very important since it affects your child's school status and graduation date.
4. Does the facility understand young people? Understanding is demonstrated by snack breaks, field trips, and similar activities. Young people need breaks from the intensity of treatment.

Your child's temperament and attitude toward treatment are important issues to consider. Decide if your child requires a locked or unlocked ward. Staff members can help you with this decision. One counselor explained, "A locked ward will prevent your child from running."

Now it's time for the old plus and minus trick. Rate each facility. Total the pluses and minuses. Include any other points you feel must be considered. Then make your decision.

Chapter 7: Treatment

EVALUATION

If you suspect your child is chemically dependent, I recommend professional evaluation. This usually includes a complete physical, a chemical history, psychological tests, and use of a chemical dependency checklist.

Evaluation takes ten days to two weeks. The time frame depends upon several factors. It takes time for the lab to process medical tests, time for clinicians to administer and evaluate psychological tests, and time for the user to admit his or her drug history.

Questions fall into these subject areas:

- frequency of use
- drugs used (including alcohol)
- drug combinations
- physical symptoms: blackouts, needle marks, infections, signs of withdrawal
- preoccupation with drugs
- consequences of using: car accidents, falling grades, poor health
- family's response to using

After evaluation, the hospital or treatment center will make a recommendation. This recommendation will be for or against treatment. Even if your child is diagnosed as a borderline chemical abuser, treatment might still be the best option.

In fact, some parents feel treatment should be a part of every secondary school curriculum. Treatment helps a child know him- or herself and gives the child coping skills for the future.

INPATIENT VS. OUTPATIENT

Treatment can be on an inpatient or outpatient basis. Inpatient treatment has three distinct advantages. First, it offers carryover which is important in getting young people to turn themselves around. Second, it's intensive. Daily work keeps them on target. Work can include writing a detailed drug history, keeping a diary, group participation, role playing, and individual therapy. Third, inpatient treatment makes it tough for your child to hop on the elevator and disappear.

LENGTH OF TREATMENT

Length of treatment depends upon the type of treatment, the cooperation of the patient, and the severity of chemical dependency. It is difficult to generalize on an average length.

Many young people spend at least one month in inpatient treatment. Staff members may recommend staying an extra week or two until the patient feels confident, or they may suggest a halfway house to ease your youngster into school and society.

All treatment begins with detoxification.

DETOXIFICATION

Detoxification is necessary before treatment can begin, because counselors can't reason with a child whose brain is polluted by chemicals. Length of detoxification depends upon four variables:

- drug(s) of choice
- using patterns
- length of use
- frequency of use

Some drugs are short-acting while others are long-acting. Marijuana is long-acting and is stored in fatty tissues. It takes a month or longer before the human body is cleansed of all the chemicals in a marijauna joint.[1]

Cocaine is a short-acting drug, so addicts use it more often to get the highs they are seeking. A rough rule of treatment is the shorter the high, the greater the addiction. Drugs that give users a quick high are also the drugs which give users a quick low. In order to avoid experiencing the lows, called bummers or depression, the user increases drug intake and frequency. With increased drug use comes increased body tolerance. Again the user increases drug intake and frequency.

Suddenly the user is chasing a moving target, frantically trying to balance drug doses and timing. This balancing act can lead to dangerous drug mixing and health deterioration.

When chemically dependent people stop using drugs, they suffer from withdrawal symptoms — physical and emotional traumas. Stomach cramps, hand tremors, and sweating are examples of physical withdrawal symptoms. Paranoia, depression, and unwarranted anxiety are symptoms of emotional withdrawal. Cocaine withdrawal includes a litany of both types of symptoms. "As clinical observations accumulate," says one authority, "the existence of a true withdrawal syndrome following cocaine use seems compelling. The depression, social withdrawal, craving, tremor, muscle pain, eating disturbance, electroencephalographic changes, and changes in sleeping patterns must be more than simply the consequence of what traditionally has been termed 'psychological dependence.' "[2]

These are example withdrawal symptoms of only one drug — cocaine. If the patient has multiple dependencies, detoxification can take weeks or months.

FAMILY GROUPS

Most treatment centers require family participation. Family members are required to attend group sessions. Participation of family members keeps them informed. It's also necessary for success because "failure to involve the family in treatment is almost certain to result in every family member — father and mother, brothers and sisters — in some way sabotaging the efforts of the treatment staff."[3]

Family participation is required for another reason. Chemical dependency has a ripple effect. One user affects all family members, relatives, friends, perhaps even strangers. Alcoholics Anonymous estimates one chemically dependent person affects four other people.

Group participation can really help. One authority says, "Parents, working together, can get help and develop cooperative plans that will move the problem toward some resolution instead of falling into destructive patterns."[4]

GROUPS

Group participation is governed by three rules which enable the group to function.

- Participants will be honest.
- Participants will maintain confidentiality.
- Participants will not resort to violence.

Honesty affects group behavior. The trust level of the group depends upon honesty. Participants get to know each other and really want to help each other.

Group leaders are honest, too. They tell participants when they're avoiding issues and answers. There's no cloaking the language. The group leader might come right out and say, "You're playing games with us. You're wasting our time because you're not being honest."

Violent behavior can damage, even cripple, a group. Thus, no violent behavior is permitted. This includes physical violence as well as verbal threats.

COMPLETION OF TREATMENT

Not all young people are dismissed from treatment. Some run away. Some are kicked out. Dismissal can include special arrangements, recommendations, and contracts.

Contracts between counselors and adolescents can be written or verbal or both. The recovering chemically dependent person agrees to meet certain standards. Agreements are based upon mutual trust. In some cases, contracts include stiff penalties: "Anaker and Crowley (1982) have adapted the behavioral method of contingency contracting . . . for cocaine use. The contract involves such contingencies as the therapist's holding letters of notification of cocaine abuse or resignation of professional licenses, written by the patient with content chosen specifically because of severe irrevocable personal effects, and mailing them to drug enforcement authorities, employers, or licensing boards upon finding evidence of cocaine use in urinalysis or after missed urinalysis."[5]

One thing is clear — counselors are rooting for your child. Dismissal day is an exciting day. Many treatment centers hold special "graduation" ceremonies in which the young people are given medallions recognizing their accomplishments.

AFTERCARE

Aftercare can last a long time. It can include psychotherapy, group therapy, vocational rehabilitation, educational rehabilitation, and family counseling. Alcoholics Anonymous says aftercare lasts for life.

During aftercare, young people can get support from groups, halfway houses, and other recovering chemically dependent people. It's comforting for children to know support is "out there." Most recovering chemically dependent people attend weekly groups. Some go twice a week. Others go daily.

Halfway houses are a practical aftercare option. A halfway house is a place where the recovering chemically dependent person lives until he or she feels ready to enter the mainstream of society. Trained counselors and group leaders are part of the management staff. You can expect management to evict any uncooperative residents of the halfway house. No individual has the right to keep others from making progress.

Unfortunately, there are not enough halfway houses to meet the demand. Many are not only full but have waiting lists.

Chapter 8: Avoid These Pitfalls

There is no good time for chemical dependency. Other family problems such as the death of a parent, career pressure, illness, and ongoing financial problems can add to your stress load.

Avoiding pitfalls can't eliminate stress. But knowing about pitfalls can help you navigate through difficult times.

DIVERSIONARY TACTICS

Kids addicted to drugs will do anything to continue using. This includes the conscious or unconscious use of diversionary tactics. Two tactics you might see are what I call "divide and conquer" and "fake problems." Both have the same purpose — to get parents fighting with each other and divert them from the real problem of chemical dependency.

Divide and Conquer

Parents are aware of their children's efforts to "play one against the other." This behavior is seen in every family and is probably prompted by the children's desire to have their own way. For most parents this is a minor irritation, but for parents of chemically dependent children it can be devastating. The already-heavy stresses of living with a chemically dependent child are burdened further when the youngster tries to protect his or her drug abuse by dividing and conquering parents.

Most parents, though shaken by this behavior, are able to withstand the added pressure on their marriage. Some, however, are not. At a midwestern hospital specializing in the treatment of chemically dependent teenagers, one couple tracked weekly changes in the group. Each week the parents' group got smaller. One couple dropped out because they were getting a divorce. A second couple dropped out because they separated. A third couple continued to attend the group sessions but argued constantly. Evidently "divide and conquer" was working.

Fake Problems

The litany of fake problems can be interesting, at times humorous, and often pitiful. Some examples of fake problems statements are

"You never listen to me."
"My teachers don't understand me."
"My bike is older than everyone else's."
"I wanted kelly green carpet in my room!"
"You always loved Susie more."
"Why do you have to be gone so much?"

Fake problems cause trouble because they contain an element of truth. These problems can also divert the group for days. A sharp counselor puts a stop to the fake problems ploy and gets the group back on target.

"None of those sentences change the facts," said one counselor. "You're here because you messed up." He paused. "You're here because you're a junkie."

PSYCHIATRISTS UNTRAINED IN CHEMICAL DEPENDENCY

Psychiatrists have great diversity in training. Some are trained to deal with chemical dependency and some are not. Psychiatrists not trained in chemical dependency often make the same mistakes parents do. They might

- deny drugs are the problem
- mistake addictive behavior for medical symptoms
- try traditional treatment on the drug-dependent child

- bargain with the user
- allow personal problems to interfere with treatment

One psychiatrist tried bargaining. "Back off the pot and I'll get your parents off your back," she said. Bargaining proved to be dangerous. Just one week later this kid overdosed and was brought into detox by worried friends.

Many parents, after learning their child is using drugs, immediately reach for the phone and call a psychiatrist. This may not be the best decision. Phyllis and David York, trained counselors themselves, explain: "We learned the traditional psychological theories in our training as [alcohol and other drug] abuse counselors and family therapists, but we came to question many of these ideas and how they are applied when we found ourselves on the other side of the counseling session in the role of troubled parents."[1]

A psychiatrist who undermines parents and enables drug use is a psychiatrist you don't need, but one who is trained in the treatment of chemical dependency and understands young people is a gem.

INCOMPETENT STAFF

Keep your eyes open! Poorly qualified people and institutions can hop on the treatment bandwagon in hopes of reaping fat profits. In some states you only need six weeks of classes to become a chemical dependency practitioner. This is hardly in-depth training for such a complex problem.

Make certain the people offering help are not only trained, but adequately trained. You should also make sure they aren't engaged in territorial disputes.

TERRITORIAL DISPUTES

Territorial disputes are interagency disputes to retain clients. Disputes are based upon politics and money. They're understandable. In order to be cost-effective, a treatment center needs to fill as many beds as possible. This is good business, but parents caught in territorial disputes find themselves in the midst of bad business. They hardly know which way to turn. They become confused by the sheer numbers of agencies and staff members involved.

My advice is let the agencies settle their own differences. Your primary concern is your child. Focus all your actions on this objective.

BIASES

As in many areas of society, you may encounter biases in the treatment maze. Biases can be based upon education, humor, intelligence, and accomplishments.

One counselor had difficulty dealing with his resentment of the father of a patient. The father, a physician, had treated chemically dependent people, and the counselor constantly chided him, losing sight of the patient and concentrating on the parent.

Another counselor kept making references to the parent's IQ. "You're obviously very intelligent," she said angrily. In this example, too, the child's welfare is at least momentarily set aside because of a bias toward a parent.

There are some counselors who are unconsciously biased against the young people sent to treatment by the courts. Many of these youngsters have criminal records and can be tough to handle; this reenforces the bias.

Parents, too, can be guilty of allowing their biases to affect their cooperation with the people who are trying to help their child.

All biases interfere with treatment.

POOR LISTENING

Listening is vital to treatment. An acquired skill, listening requires patience and energy. Current communications texts refer to *good* listening as *active* listening.

During active listening the body actually becomes more active. The heart rate accelerates and body temperature rises slightly. Both changes demonstrate that listening requires physical effort.

Active listeners not only listen for facts, they listen for feelings. An active listener

- listens *with* the speaker
- tries to understand the speaker's connotation of words
- listens to nonverbal communication
- listens to what *isn't* being said and to what is
- listens attentively[2]

Good chemical dependency counselors have these qualities. But don't assume *all* counselors have them. A classic example of poor listening was the counselor who prescribed treatment before hearing the facts. This is like prescribing medication before hearing the symptoms. Not surprisingly, this counselor proved to be harmful.

JARGON

The dictionary defines jargon as incoherent speech, gibberish, a language or dialect that is incomprehensible, outlandish, or a specialized vocabulary. Parents who are unfamiliar with chemical dependency jargon quickly agree it is incomprehensible.

Soon parents are suffering from jargon glut. Well-meaning counselors use so much jargon, parents can't decode it and become confused. They can't tell what's going on. They don't know what is expected of them.

As one expert on teenage chemical dependency drew arrows on the chalkboard to illustrate descriptions of drugged behavior, one mother turned to another. Wide-eyed, she asked, "What on earth is she trying to tell us?" Neither mother knew the answer.

Chemically dependent children try to fool their parents by using jargon too. Don't be intimidated by it.

TAKING ON OTHER PEOPLE'S THOUGHTS

Treatment makes you vulnerable. Weeks of gut-level honesty, anxiety, and sadness take their toll. To add to your burdens, people who don't even know you, freely hand out advice. For example, they may say

"You should go to more groups."
"You should read a historical novel."
"Take up a new hobby."

Maybe you don't want to do any of these things. Who wants to go to more evening meetings? Who has the patience to read a historical novel? Who has time to take up a new hobby?

One resource some parents have found helpful is *Feeling Good* by David D. Burns, M.D. Basically, Dr. Burns says you have psychiatric rights. You also have the power to influence your psyche. Reading Burn's book may help parents take some special advice — their own.

Instead of a parade of evening meetings, you may choose to stay home and rest. Instead of plodding through historical novels, you may decide to read science fiction. Instead of starting a new hobby, you may choose to return to the comfort of an old hobby.

Don't take on anybody else's thoughts. Be your own person.

CHANGE OF LOCATION SOLUTION

Some parents look for a simple answer, a quick bandage for their child's problem. The change of location solution is one of these. These parents believe if they send their child to a private church school, or to an exclusive school, or to visit a distant relative, chemical dependency will leave their house.

"Our children are enrolled in parochial school so they won't get into drugs," a mother announced confidently. She obviously hadn't heard the school district's chemical dependency counselor speak. (The top drug-using school was that school.) And the counselor had explained that all schools were affected by chemical dependency, and were "taking turns" in having the highest rate of use.

The change of location solution ignores the facts of chemical dependency. The school or city is not chemically dependent; the child is. And that child will bring the same using behaviors to a new school or city.

TOO MUCH EDUCATION

Parents respond to their children's chemical dependency in a variety of ways. One mother, a nurse, immediately enrolled in a counselor training course. Another took out dozens of books from city and college libraries on the subject of chemical dependency. A third attended virtually every support group in town.

These are the responses of loving and worried parents. However, none of these responses provides the professional help your child needs. Course work, extended reading, and group participation require vast time and energy. This time and energy might best be spent in the treatment process itself.

Keep this in mind: You don't need to know all there is to help your child.

GUILT FEELINGS

Right after the shock wave comes the guilt wave. Guilt can hit with gale force. Perhaps you feel guilty because you're employed. This guilt trip can really get to you, especially if you're a woman. "Should I have stayed home and been a full-time mother?" you may ask.

Perhaps you feel guilty because you just received a promotion. You can hardly enjoy the accomplishment if you're wondering, "Is my child intimidated by my success?"

Perhaps you feel guilty about parenting. You may feel that you have failed because you have a chemically dependent child. "Where did I go wrong?" you might ask.

Perhaps you feel guilty about your role model in the community. Everyone knows you, your husband, your child. You might ask yourself, "What will the neighbors think?"

Perhaps you feel guilty about the times *you* drank too much. You worry about your child and yourself. "Am I an alcoholic?" you may wonder.

Perhaps you even feel guilty about not feeling guilty enough. This seems to be ridiculous, yet it can be very real. Keep in mind "drug abusers tend to project most of the blame onto their parents without accepting ultimate responsibility for their own behavior."[3] Don't waste time on guilt.

DEPRESSION

Roller-coaster emotions can easily lead to depression. Parents of chemically dependent children resemble the walking wounded. Talk to other parents and they'll tell you they mourned their child. It was as if their child had died. Stages of grief progressed through denial, anger, bargaining, depression, and finally acceptance.

Some parents mourn an actual death. I know of one couple whose teenage son committed suicide. These parents continue to attend group sessions, trying to come to grips with what happened and trying to help other parents.

Bear in mind there's a big difference between sadness and depression: "The distinction is simple. Sadness is a normal emotion created by realistic perceptions that describe a negative event involving loss or disappointment in an undistorted way. Depression is an illness that *always* results from thoughts that are distorted in some way."[4]

Try to identify which you are feeling — sadness or depression. Once you know what's bothering you, you'll be better able to handle it.

Chapter 9: Survival Tips

Your child's treatment can dominate your life. It's with you every hour of the day and may disrupt your sleep at night. Painful discoveries about a child's behavior add to your worries. Discoveries can include stealing, dealing, abortion, prostitution, and connections with organized crime. No wonder parents have trouble sleeping. Participating in regular family groups is tiring. How do you survive this time?

Take Care of Yourself

Ask yourself, "Who is the best person to take care of me?" The answer is easy — you. Therefore, decide to do the things you know are best for you.

Get enough sleep. If you didn't sleep through the night, be grateful for the sleep you did get. No moaning and groaning about lost hours; that just makes you feel worse. Work on perfecting the art of catnapping.

Eat regular meals. You've probably been chomping on junk food. Bypass the fast-food joints. Try to eat balanced meals. And, if you can, go out for dinner once in a while.

Look your best. This sounds simple, but it's true. You feel better if you look your best. Take time for haircuts, shopping for and coordinating clothing.

Join a Group

Parallel to the growth of chemical dependency has come the growth of support groups. Public schools, churches, and treatment centers all have support groups for parents. Independent groups (parents banding together) are springing up all across the country.

Should you join a support group? Decide what works for you. Attend a meeting. If the group helps you, join it.

Your family may act as a support group: grandparents, aunts, uncles, distant relatives, and in-laws. If you think including family members is too big a burden for them or you, don't do it.

Handle Stress

Treatment is time-consuming. It's almost like having two lives. Merging your treatment life and your regular life can put you on overload. Careful planning is one way to combat stress.

"To do" lists and calendar entries are two kinds of planning which help harried parents. These lists can be subdivided into errands, household maintenance, and treatment. Don't get too involved with the lists. Keep them short and simple.

Calendar entries include both scheduled appointments as well as appointment reminders. These advance reminders, called a Tic or Tickler file, ensure things will get done.

Your ear probably hurts from making so many phone calls. All the numbers are merging in your mind. Well, the phone calls can't be avoided. However, you can help yourself by keeping calls straight. Hang or tape a list of treatment-related numbers next to the phone. Record calls as you make them. When the phone bills come you'll be able to account for them quickly.

Exercise

Physicians have long known exercise helps combat stress. "It doesn't have to hurt to be helpful," explains one doctor. "Find something that is fun."

The word exercise isn't synonymous with the word expensive. Walking is one of the best forms of exercise and gets you out of the house. An exercise bike allows you to exercise while watching TV. Joining a bowling league provides weekly contact with friends.

Whatever type of exercise you choose, physicians recommend regular exercise.

Talk With Other Parents

You may not be able to or wish to handle this alone. You can confide in friends and relatives. Simply verbalizing what has been happening to you will help. Perhaps you want to arrange regular coffee klatches with a special friend. "In our experience," say Phyllis and David York, "we found that without our heavy reliance on our friends we could have easily slipped back into our old [behavior] patterns."[1]

Set Reasonable Goals

Be kind to yourself during this trying time. Don't set unreasonable goals. Concentrate on what you get done in a day, not what you don't get done.

So supper doesn't rate four stars — so what. So you didn't get the cleaning done — so what. So you're behind on the laundry — so what. Most problems are small when compared to chemical dependency.

In an effort to get the household chores done, a mother assigned laundry duty to her teenage son. He did the laundry — sporatically. The mother stuck to her guns. She said, philosophically, "It's amazing how long kids can sleep on dirty sheets." It seems her son didn't like sleeping on dirty sheets as much as he thought. Laundry was soon being done on a regular basis.

Reward Yourself

Rewarding yourself is an extension of kindness. Naturally, one person's reward might be another person's penance.

One father wanted to go trout fishing. His wife's reaction? "Yuk." Their solution was to give each other space. He went fishing, rod and reel in hand, while she stayed home and read magazines. They were both happy.

You can also reward yourself with a gift. Have you wanted that striped shirt for weeks? Want no more. Buy it. You'll find the reward makes you feel better all day. If you bought the shirt on sale, it could make you feel better all week.

Get Away

Getting away for a few hours, or days, or weeks, can make things seem brighter. Recognize getting away for what it is — a breather. It is *not* a form of the change of location solution.

Perhaps you feel you don't have the money to get away; the bank balance is depleted due to mounting treatment costs. Getting away doesn't have to be expensive. It can be as simple as a backyard barbecue or as complex as a trip.

Choose an option which meets your mental and physical needs. Getting away can be passive, slightly active, or very active.

Reading magazines at the library, watching a movie, listening to a public radio concert are examples of passive options. Attending an art exhibit, lunching with a friend, or taking a walk are examples of more active options. Swimming at an exercise club, playing in a softball league, canoeing through white water are examples of active options.

Whichever option you choose, make it hassle-free. Getting away shouldn't put you away.

Chapter 10: Just When You Think You're Done

Your child's completion of treatment doesn't mean you're done. Treatment often falters during aftercare. Reasons for this are varied but include fatigue, depression, dwindling funds, and other children experimenting with drugs.

It's important to hang on. Don't give up!

RECOVERY PHASES

Even though your child has been through treatment, the recovery process continues. Recovery isn't instantaneous. Children progress through several recovery phases.

- Right after treatment many recovering chemically dependent people feel euphoria. They accepted the treatment challenge. They did it!
- After euphoria, depression can set in. Away from the treatment facility, the recovering person has time to think about what has happened.
- Next comes the soapbox syndrome. The recovering person is out to save the world, telling anybody and everybody about the dangers of using.
- Finally, emotions level off and the recovering person really faces reality. This leveling-off process can take months, even years.

As you watch your child pass through these recovery stages, watch yourself also. Parents often progress through the same recovery stages.

IMMATURITY

You might notice that your child, although now straight, doesn't seem to be mature. Compared with other children, he or she doesn't act the same age. This is because no maturation takes place while kids are on drugs. "It seems to us," say Phyllis and David York, "that drugs tend to keep young people resentful, grudging infants."[1]

Tally the number of months or years your child was using drugs and you'll have a concept of how much maturation lies ahead. This is a time when parents have to be patient. Nobody matures overnight.

SPECIAL PROGRAMS

Parents might want to design a living program for their child. A social worker can help with this. Rules should be simple, but effective. One couple designed this program in conjunction with their daughter, a senior high school student. She would do the following:

1. LIVE ON HER OWN. This stipulation gave the daughter practical, day-to-day living experience.
2. RECEIVE A MONTHLY STIPEND. Parents agreed to pay the same stipend their daughter would have received on welfare.
3. PURCHASE OWN FOOD. This stipulation helped sharpen the daughter's budgeting skills.
4. BE RESPONSIBLE FOR OWN TRANSPORTATION. Parents would no longer supply the use of the car, with gas, or "taxi" service.
5. RECEIVE MEDICAL CARE. Parents agreed to pay all medical bills. If the child became very ill, parents would provide transportation to and from the physician.
6. PARTICIPATE IN AFTERCARE GROUPS. Selection of these groups was left up to the daughter, under supervision of a social worker.

Sit down with your child and discuss what would be mutually beneficial. All parties should benefit. "TOUGHLOVE does *not* encourage parents to 'throw their kids out of the house.' Only after other alternatives are attempted is an acting-out youth faced with a *structured choice* to change his or her behavior or leave."[2]

LIVING WITH THE RESULTS

After a child completes treatment, parents may feel bewildered. Intellectually, they can hardly process what has happened. They are emotionally drained. Whether treatment is successful or not, parents must live with the results.

Counselors tell parents treatment "doesn't always take." At one Minneapolis treatment center a fifteen year old enrolled for her eighth try at treatment. Unfortunately, she didn't finish. She ran away.

Why does treatment fail? It's difficult to pinpoint reasons, but two possibilities are the timing could be wrong or the treatment center might not be the right one for your child.

Timing. Your child might not be ready for treatment. Instead, your child might have to experience more consequences of using and more pain. Some facilities refer to this as "bottoming out."

Wrong treatment type/center. No chemical dependency facility guarantees success. Neither the facility nor the staff are God. Perhaps you selected the wrong type of treatment or the wrong center. You might want to do more research on chemical dependency facilities and suggest treatment again.

OPTIONS

Your child may still think a little using is an option — a couple of joints or a few beers with the gang won't hurt. Alcoholics Anonymous' premise of total abstinence works. Before treatment is successful, your child may have to admit using is no longer an option.

Success or failure of treatment is your child's responsibility, not yours. Console yourself with the fact that you did the best you could at the time. That's all any parent can do. The following incident illustrates this point.

Two medical professionals, a doctor and a nurse, met on the elevator one morning. They hadn't seen each other for two years. Each had participated, along with their children, in a drug awareness program for teens. "How are you doing?" the doctor asked.

The nurse replied, "I'm divorced from my husband. He's still a practicing alcoholic. My oldest child is still straight. My middle child is still experimenting. My youngest is still a junkie." She smiled. "Surprisingly, I'm happy. I know I did all I could."

Chapter 11: Getting On With Your Life

You've spent considerable time thinking about your child. Now it's time to think about yourself. As one social worker said to a mother, "Get on with your life!" This sentence is easy to say and often difficult to do.

After treatment many parents can't seem to "get going." They constantly feel tired. So much energy has been spent on their child, they have little left for themselves.

Some parents feel a resurgence of guilt. Working mothers, in particular, may feel guilty about setting career goals. Parents may feel guilty about spending time together and enjoying themselves. Finishing dinner in a well-known restaurant, a wife commented to her husband, "I feel guilty about having fun." At least she could identify her feelings. Some parents can't.

Before making any decisions about the future, you must ask yourself two important questions. "Where have I come from?" "Where am I going?"

TAKING STOCK: WHERE HAVE I COME FROM?

The first question involves sorting out feelings from facts. This is a difficult process. As you answer the questions, you need to do three kinds of thinking.

Discard Psychological Baggage

Cast aside the hundreds of details which crowd your mind. Discard expensive car accidents, lost or bartered goods, hurting words which have been exchanged. Naturally, discarding details doesn't imply you have forgotten them. The human mind, the ultimate computer, has stored all these details. However, you can make a conscious effort to minimize them.

Emphasize the Positives

Focus on positive thinking. Think of the skills you acquired during treatment, of the friends you have made. List them on paper to get a clear picture. Perhaps you learned how to participate in groups, prioritize, handle stress, fine-tune listening skills, interpret body language, manage time efficiently, do quick research, deal with anger in positive ways, and demonstrate love openly and freely. All of these skills can be used.

Take Action

Opposite each skill, list a way in which the skill could be used. Really brainstorm. List practical and fanciful ideas. Now pick one skill and work on it. Your aim is to turn observation into reality. Make something positive happen!

MAKING PLANS: WHERE AM I GOING?

This question requires more time to answer. It involves the aftertreatment role model. This role model is important for all family members. Children need to see their parents leading active lives. Parents need to feel as if they are in charge of their lives.

When time comes full circle and the child returns asking for advice (he or she probably will), the child finds interesting and growing parents.

Getting Out Into the Community

You say you're ready to get out into the community? Hooray! You say you're scared to get out into the community? Okay. Some fear of social contact is normal after family treatment.

Many parents experience a loss of self-confidence. Although the loss is usually temporary, it's still devastating. Loss of self-confidence is magnified by the casual comments of friends.

"You're a tough act to follow!" one talented mother was told. Not only did she hear this once, she heard it repeatedly. The comment hurt. Why? Because it placed blame for the child's chemical dependency upon the parent, instead of the child.

Grit your teeth and ignore these kinds of comments. They can render you "null and void." Realize the comments are made out of ignorance by people who don't understand addiction or treatment.

Certainly, you can't become a nonperson, hiding your talents and feeling guilty about them. You are who you are. Perhaps now is the time to try a new hobby, join a club, or take a trip. There's lots more living to do.

Summary

You've reached the end — which is really the beginning. This book has given you a glimpse of what to expect during the course of treatment. This book is not insurance. It cannot keep your child from harm or you from pain. If this is your first exposure to the subject of chemical dependency, your brain is on overload. Put the book away for a few days. Read it again after your subconscious has processed the information.

Discuss the book with family and friends. Only by reaching out to each other will we be able to help ourselves and others whose lives are affected by drugs. After you've discussed the book, do something!

Mothers Against Driving Drunk (MADD) and similar groups are having an effect on teenage drug use. The young people themselves are getting involved, creating SADD (Students Against Driving Drunk) and signing contracts against driving drunk. In some cities parents have banded together, adhering to a standard code of conduct and curfew hours. The National Institute on Drug Abuse is waging its "Just Say No" campaign via buttons, brochures, and TV ads. While these steps are helping, more needs to be done.

- Parents need to be informed.
- Parents need to organize.
- Parents need to communicate.

This book evolved from an article about chemical dependency I wrote for a local magazine. No sooner had the magazine hit the newsstands than the phone started ringing. Callers' comments were similar, but one comment affected me deeply.

A mother described how she felt closed in a closet, nowhere to turn, and completely isolated. "Thank you for speaking out," she said. "I thought I stood all alone."

Parents are not alone. Help is available for you and your child. This book is an initial link in the "help chain." Will you do me a favor? When you're through with the book, pass it on. Maybe it can help someone else.

REFERENCES

Chapter 1

[1]Lloyd Johnson, Patrick O'Malley, and Jerald Bachman, *Drugs and American High School Students 1975-1983* (Rockville, MD, National Institute on Drug Abuse, 1984), p. 11.

[2]Ibid., p. 20.

[3]Lowell Ponte, "Deadly Mixers: Alcohol and Tobacco," *Reader's Digest*, (April, 1985), p. 53.

[4]Joseph Brady and Scott Lukas, eds., *Testing Drugs for Physical Dependence Potential and Abuse Liability* (Rockville, MD, National Institute on Drug Abuse, 1984), p. 4.

[5]John Grabowski, ed., *Cocaine: Pharmacology, Effects, and Treatment of Abuse* (Rockville, MD, National Institute on Drug Abuse, 1984), p. 95.

[6]Frank Scarpitti and Susan Datesman, *Drugs and the Youth Culture* (Beverly Hills, CA, Sage Publications, Inc., 1980), p. 300.

Chapter 2

[1]George G. Comerci, "Spotting the Young Substance Abuser in Your Practice," *Diagnosis*, March, 1985, p. 78.

[2]Ibid., p. 78.

[3]Lloyd Johnson, Patrick O'Malley, and Jerald Bachman, *Drugs and American High School Students 1975-1983*, (Rockville, MD, National Institute on Drug Abuse, 1984), p. 60.

Chapter 3

[1]J. William Langston, "The Case of the Tainted Heroin," *M.D. Magazine*, (March, 1985), p. 108.

[2]Ibid., p. 198.

[3]Ira Mothner and Alan Weitz, *How to Get Off Drugs* (New York, Simon and Schuster, 1984), pp. 227-228.

[4]Frank Scarpitti and Susan Datesman, *Drugs and the Youth*

Culture (Beverly Hills, CA, Sage Publications, Inc., 1980), p. 296.

Chapter 5

[1]Frank Scarpitti and Susan Datesman, *Drugs and the Youth Culture* (Beverly Hills, CA, Sage Publications, Inc., 1980), p. 218.

[2]Peggy Mann, *How Much Do You Really Know About Marijuana?* (New York, Woodmere Press).

[3]Lloyd Johnston, Patrick O'Malley, and Jerald Bachman, *Drugs and American High School Students 1975-1983* (Rockville, MD, National Institute on Drug Abuse, 1984), p. 108.

[4]Oakley Ray, *Drugs, Society and Human Behavior* (St. Louis, MO, The C. V. Mosby Co., 1983), p. 459.

Chapter 6

[1]John Grabowski, ed., *Cocaine: Pharmacology, Effects, and Treatment of Abuse* (Rockville, MD, National Institute on Drug Abuse, 1984), p. 12.

[2]Muriel James and Dorothy Jongeward, *Born to Win* (Phillipines, Addison-Wesley Publishing Co., 1971), p. 8.

[3]Eric Berne, *Transactional Analysis in Psychotherapy* (New York, Ballantine Books, 1961), p. 3.

[4]James and Jongeward, p. 11.

[5]Ibid., p. 11.

[6]Richard Price *et al.*, *Principles of Psychology* (New York, Holt, Rinehart and Winston, 1982), p. 460.

[7]David Burns, *Feeling Good* (New York, William Morrow, 1980), p. 24.

[8]Price *et al.*, p. 460.

[9]Ibid., p. 460.

[10]Frank Scarpitti and Susan Datesman, *Drugs and the Youth Culture* (Beverly Hills, CA, Sage Publications, Inc., 1980), pp. 291-292.

Chapter 7

[1]Peggy Mann, *How Much Do You Really Know About Marijuana?* (New York, Woodmere Press).

[2]John Grabowski, ed., *Cocaine: Pharmacology, Effects, and Treatment of Abuse* (Rockville, MD, National Institute on Drug Abuse, 1984), p. 47.

[3]Frank Scarpitti and Susan Datesman, *Drugs and the Youth Culture* (Beverly Hills, CA, Sage Publications, Inc., 1980), p. 302.

[4]Phyllis York, David York, and Ted Wachtel, *TOUGHLOVE* (Garden City, Doubleday & Co., 1982), p. 15.

[5]Grabowski, p. 115.

Chapter 8

[1]Phyllis York, David York, and Ted Wachtel, *TOUGHLOVE* (Garden City, Doubleday & Co., 1982), p. 23.

[2]Norman Sigband and David Bateman, *Communicating in Business* (Scott, Foresman and Co., 1981), Chapter 4.

[3]Frank Scarpitti and Susan Datesman, *Drugs and the Youth Culture* (Beverly Hills, CA, Sage Publications, Inc., 1980), p. 302.

[4]David Burns, *Feeling Good* (New York, William Morrow, 1980), p. 205.

Chapter 9

[1]Phyllis York, David York, and Ted Wachtel, *TOUGHLOVE* (Garden City, Doubleday & Co., 1982), p. 117.

Chapter 10

[1]Phyllis York, David York, and Ted Wachtel, *TOUGHLOVE* (Garden City, Doubleday & Co., 1982), p. 39.

[2]Ibid., p. 19.

READING LIST

Berne, Eric, *Transactional Analysis in Psychotherapy*, New York, Ballantine Books, 1961.

Brady, Joseph, and Scott Lukas, eds., *Testing Drugs for Physical Dependence Potential and Abuse Liability*, Rockville, MD, National Institute on Drug Abuse, 1984.

Burns, David, *Feeling Good*, New York, William Morrow, 1980.

Comerci, George G., "Spotting the Young Substance Abuser in Your Practice," *Diagnosis*, March, 1985.

Dulfano, Celia, *Families, Alcoholism, and Recovery*, Center City, MN, Hazelden Educational Materials, 1982.*

Grabowski, John, *Cocaine: Pharmacology, Effects, and Treatment of Abuse*, Rockville, MD, National Institute on Drug Abuse, 1984.

H., Barbara, *Untying the Knots*, Center City, MN, Hazelden Educational Materials, 1984.*

Hancock, David C., D.D., *Points for Parents Perplexed About Drugs*, Center City, MN, Hazelden Educational Materials, 1975.*

James, Muriel, and Dorothy Jongeward, *Born to Win*, Philippines, Addison-Wesley Publishing Co., 1971.

Johnston, Lloyd, Patrick O'Malley, and Jerald Bachman, *Drugs and American High School Students 1975-1983*, Rockville, MD, National Institute on Drug Abuse, 1984.

Keller, John E., *Alcohol: A Family Affair*, The Kroc Foundation, Santa Ynez, CA, 1977.*

Krupski, Ann Marie, *Inside the Adolescent Alcoholic*, Hazelden Educational Materials, 1982.*

LaFountain, William, *Setting Limits*, Center City, MN, Hazelden Educational Materials, 1982.*

Lajtha, Abel, ed., *Handbook of Neurochemistry*, Vol. 10, Ch. 22, New York, Plenum Press, 1985.

Langston, J. William, "The Case of the Tainted Heroin," *M.D. Magazine*, March, 1985.

Lawson, Gary, James Peterson, and Ann Lawson, *Alcoholism*

and the Family, Rockville, MD, Aspen Systems Corporation, 1983.

Mann, Peggy, *How Much Do You Really Know About Marijuana?* New York, Woodmere Press, n.d.

Mothner, Ira, and Alan Weitz, *How to Get Off Drugs*, New York, Simon and Schuster, 1984.

Perkins, William Mack, and Nancy McMurtrie-Perkins, *Raising Drug-Free Kids in a Drug-Filled World*, Center City, MN, Hazelden Educational Materials, 1986.*

Ponte, Lowell, "Deadly Mixers: Alcohol and Tobacco," *Reader's Digest*, April 1985, pp. 53-54.

Price, Richard, Mitchell Glickstein, David Horton, and Ronald Bailey, *Principles of Psychology*, New York, Holt, Rinehart and Winston, 1982.

Ray, Oakley, *Drugs, Society and Human Behavior*, St. Louis, MO, The C. V. Mosby Co., 1983.

Scarpitti, Frank, and Susan Datesman, *Drugs and the Youth Culture*, Beverly Hills, CA, Sage Publications, Inc., 1980.

Sigband, Norman, and David Bateman, *Communicating in Business*, Scott, Foresman and Co., 1981.

Tims, Frank, and Jacqueline Ludford, eds., *Drug Abuse Treatment: Strategies, Progress, and Prospects*, Rockville, MD, National Institute on Drug Abuse, 1984.

Wegscheider, Don, *If Only My Family Understood Me . . .*, Minneapolis, CompCare Publications, 1979.

York, Phyllis, David York, and Ted Wachtel, *TOUGHLOVE*, Garden City, New York, Doubleday & Co., 1982.

---

*Available from Hazelden Educational Materials, Box 176, Center City, MN 55012-0176. (1-800-328-9000)

Hazelden

Other titles that will interest you...

Kids, Drugs, and the Law
by David G. Evans, Esq.

Can a minor consent to chemical dependency treatment? Are parents liable for their children's private or civil misdeeds? Attorney and author David G. Evans answers these questions and more. This highly informative book will help parents understand the legal rights and responsibilities of kids who use alcohol and other drugs. (88 pp.)
Order No. 1341

When A Bough Breaks
A Novel by Mary Ylvisaker Nilsen

A poignant novel that will touch the heart of anyone who has a chemically dependent family member. *When A Bough Breaks* follows a family through a five day family treatment program and relates the dramatic changes they experience. Of special interest to teens, parents, children of alcoholics, and anyone who has been through a family program. (220 pp.)
Order No. 5090

Inside the Adolescent Alcoholic
by Ann Marie Krupski

"Once a young person becomes addicted to alcohol, the normal distress of adolescence is accentuated and distorted in a whirlwind of alcohol-induced confusion." This book explores the vulnerability of adolescence, the destructive behaviors that arise from adolescent addiction, and the parallel struggles of parents. (80 pp.)
Order No. 1077

For price and order information, please call one of our Customer Service Representatives.

Hazelden
Educational Materials ®

Pleasant Valley Road
Box 176
Center City, MN 55012-0176

(800) 328-9000
(Toll Free. U.S. Only)

(800) 257-0070
(Toll Free. MN Only)

(612) 257-4010
(Alaska and Outside U.S.)